The Moscow Kremlii

Text Irina Polynina,
Irina Rodimtseva

Photography
Nikolai Rakhmanov

Translation Kate Cook-Horujy

Red Square Publishers Moscow 2000

Introduction

The Moscow Kremlin is a unique monument of history and culture with its splendid creations of architecture and art.

The Kremlin has always been the focal point of the growth of the Russian state, the stage of many dramatic and glorious events. This architectural ensemble of rare beauty and character grew up gradually over the centuries. It is rightly called a "chronicle in stone".

The first entries in this chronicle were made in 1147 by Prince Yuri Dologoruky (the Long-Armed) who ruled Moscow which then covered only a part of the territory of the present Kremlin. Burnt down by the Mongol-Tatars in 1238, Moscow recovered and continued to grow. The oak walls of the Kremlin erected by Prince Ivan Kalita (the Moneybag) around 1340 defended what was now the capital city of a principality which included many of the Russian lands. The first Assumption Cathedral erected in the Kremlin, a very small one, was built at the same time. The cathedral later became the main church of Russian Orthodoxy.

The white-stone walls of the Kremlin erected in 1366–1367 issued a challenge to the powerful Mongol-Tatar overlords. An army assembled from the various Russian lands and led by Prince Dmitri Donskoy of Moscow marched out from the Kremlin against the Mongol-Tatars, and his victory in the Battle of Kulikovo of 1380 laid the foundations for the liberation of Russia from foreign dominion. The walls erected under Ivan III at the end of the fifteenth century were a symbol of the final collapse of this foreign overlordship.

When he became an "autocrat", i.e., the head of a powerful, independent state, Ivan III began a large-scale building programme in the Kremlin. As well as fortified walls and towers, he built the magnificent Hall of Facets, a new Assumption Cathedral, the Archangel and Annunciation cathedrals, the Church of the Deposition of the Robe and the Ivan the Great Bell-Tower. This formed the splendid architectural ensemble in Cathedral Square, which at that time was completed in the south by the Treasury Court where the grand prince's valuables were kept.

Ivan IV's adoption of the title of tsar was an important landmark in the history of Russia. He was crowned tsar in the Assumption Cathedral in 1547. In the same year the chronicle mentions the Armoury. This now contains the collection of royal treasures and is the oldest Russian museum. Under Ivan IV the Russian state began to drive out its former overlords, the successors of the Mongol-Tatars. The world-famous Cathedral of St Basil's (or Church of the Intercession-on-the-Moat which is its official name) was erected by the Saviour (then Florov) Gate to commemorate the taking of Kazan.

Building the Kremlin walls in 1367. Miniature from the 16th-century Illuminated Chronicle

The Russian people's struggle for national independence at the beginning of the seventeenth century ended in 1612 with the liberation of the Kremlin from the supporters of the foreign tsar, the son of the king of Poland. The country recovered rapidly and already by 1625 the Saviour Tower acquired new tiers and a characteristic silhouette quite unlike that of other fortified structures.

In the decades that followed the architecture of the Kremlin was enriched by such buildings as the royal Terem Palace and palace churches and the Poteshny Palace. The Patriarchal Palace was completely rebuilt.

Procession by the Saviour Gate in Red Square. Miniature from the "Book on the Election to the Most High Throne... of the Sovereign, Tsar and Grand Prince Michael, son of Theodore...". 1672–1673

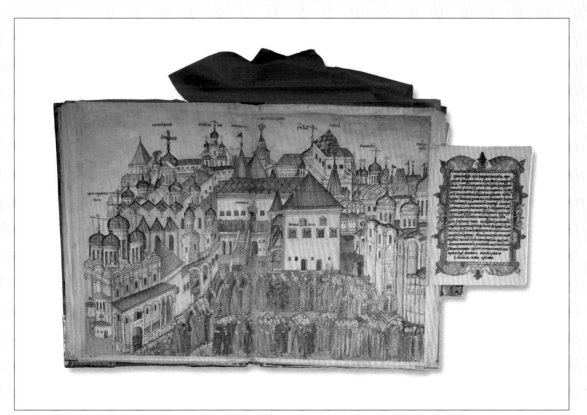

Procession into the Assumption Cathedral on the day of Tsar Michael's Coronation. Miniature from the "Book on the Election to the Most High Throne ... of the Sovereign, Tsar and Grand Prince Michael, son of Theodore..."

№30 Видъ въ проспектѣ Успенской соборной церькви и передъ оной площади и прочему спросшно

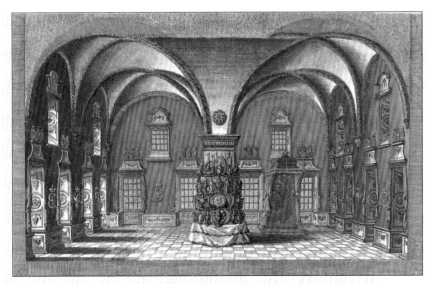

Hall of Facets. Engraving, watercolour. I.A.Sokolov. 1744. Sheet from the album "A detailed descripti- on...of the Sacred Coronation... of the Empress Elizabeth, daughter of Peter...on 25 April, 1742"

View of the Square in front of the Assumption Cathedral. Engraving, watercolour. I.A. Sokolov. 1744. Sheet from the album "A detailed description...of the Sacred Coronation...of the Empress Elizabeth, daughter of Peter...on 25 April, 1742"

When the new Russian capital, St Petersburg, was built in the reign of Peter the Great, Moscow still remained a most important centre of state government, and the Kremlin continued to be a place where many administrative buildings were concentrated, such as the Treasury Court, the prikaz (government department) buildings of 1591 and 1675–1680, Arsenal and Matvei Kazakov's unexcelled masterpiece known as the Senate (1776–1787), which is now the Residence of the Russian President.

The war of 1812 was a bitter one for Russia. Napoleon even succeeded, albeit it not for long, in taking Moscow. As they retreated the enemy blew up several buildings and towers in the Kremlin, which were restored after the Russian army entered Paris.

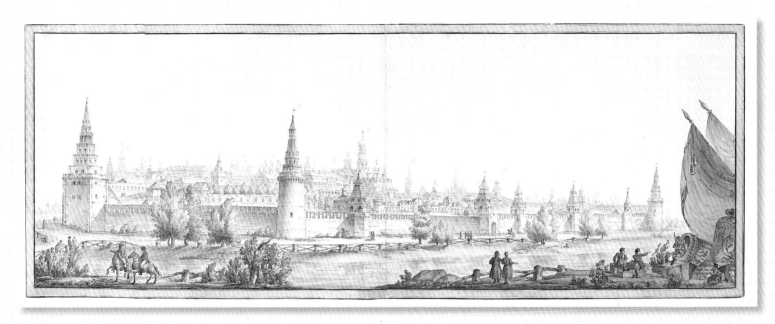

Kremlin Panorama. Watercolour.
Giacomo Quarenghi

*View of the city of Moscow taken
from the balcony of the Imperial
Palace facing left. Lithograph after a
drawing by Gerard de la Barthe.
1799*

ПАНОРАМА МОСКВЫ
во время коронации

View of St Basil's and the Saviour Gate from the Minin and Pozharsky Monument in Red Square. Watercolour. Unknown artist. 1840s

Москва

ВИДЪ СПАССКОЙ БАШНИ   VUE DE LA PORTE SAINTE

View inside the Kremlin from the Saviour Tower. Lithograph, watercolour. J.-B.Arnout. From Joseph Daziaro's "Views of Moscow". Late 1840s–early 1850s

The year 1818 saw the birth in the Kremlin of Alexander II, the emperor who abolished serfdom, an autocrat who from the heights of his throne carried out transformations that filled the sails of the Russian state with fresh breezes. In the reign of his father, Nicholas I, the Great Kremlin Palace was erected in the Kremlin, a true monument to the greatness of Imperial Russia.

PANORAMA DE MOSCOU

Kremlin Panorama during the Coronation of Alexander II. Detail. Chromolithograph. 1856

Nicholas Palace in the Kremlin. Lithograph, watercolour. Philippe Benoist, Aubrun after an original by D.S.Indeitsev. Sheet from a panorama of the Kremlin and Zamoskvorechye from the Tainitsky Tower. 1850s

In March 1918 Moscow became the capital once more, and the Kremlin the residence of supreme power, which remained there even in 1941, when the German army reached the approaches to Moscow. Enemy planes were only ten minutes away from Red Square where on 7 November, 1941 Joseph Stalin addressed the forces lined up for the traditional parade to mark the anniversary of the October revolution. In less than four years' time the troops that had defeated Germany marched over Red Square in a victory parade and the banners of the vanquished enemy were cast down at the base of the mausoleum.

For centuries the Kremlin has been the centre and symbol of the Russian state. It was always the finest Russian and foreign architects who were invited here to create and preserve an historical and architectural complex unlike any other in Europe. This was universally recognised when in 1990 the Moscow Kremlin, with its buildings from the 14th to the 20th centuries was included by UNESCO in the World Cultural and Natural Heritage List.

Walls and towers

More than eight centuries have passed since the Kremlin, the ancient fortress that marked the beginning of the city of Moscow, was built on Borovitsky Hill.

The approaches to the fortress were protected by the River Moskva in the south and the River Neglinnaya in the west. In the reign of Ivan Kalita (Moneybag) the first timber fortifications were replaced by walls and towers of oak and under Dmitri Donskoy the Kremlin became a fortress of white stone. The walls and towers that you see today were erected for the most part in the 1480s and 1490s, when a magnificent new Kremlin designed by Italian architects was built in the reign of Ivan III. They were completed in 1495, demarcating the territory of the Kremlin as it is today.

The Kremlin walls that encircle Borovitsky Hill run for 2.235 km along the River Moskva, the Alexandrovsky Gardens and Red Square. They are from 3.5 to 6.5 metres thick and from 5 to 19 metres high, depending on the relief. The walls and towers were constructed in keeping with the latest military technology.

South wall of the Kremlin from the Water to Beklemishev towers

Tainitsky Tower and Archangel Cathedral domes

A firing platform up to 4.5 metres wide runs along the top of the walls, protected by merlons with slit embrasures. There are nineteen towers altogether along the walls and one more, the twentieth, before the Trinity bridge.

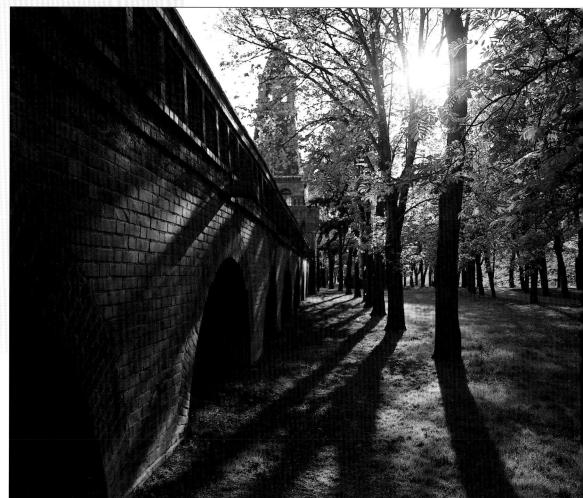

South Kremlin wall. View from the
Tainitsky Gardens

Kremlin embankment and Vasilievsky Slope

South Kremlin wall. View from the Tainitsky Gardens

Two of the corner towers on the Kremlin, which is in the form of a triangle, are cylindrical, and the third is sixteen-edged. The rest are rectangular. The corner towers each contained a well. Six towers were carriageways and had a portcullis. The only surviving portcullis is in front of the Kutafia Tower erected in 1516 opposite the Trinity Gate. The spires of the Saviour, Nicholas, Borovitsky and Trinity towers are topped with double-headed eagles, the coat-of-arms of the Russian Empire. In 1935 the eagles were replaced by five-pointed stars with semi-precious stones, which in turn were replaced two years later by luminiscent stars made of ruby-coloured glass, one also being added to the Water Tower. Each star weighs more than a ton, and they range from 3 to 3.75 metres in diameter.

One of the most beautiful Kremlin towers is the Saviour Tower. It was used for the most solemn processions of the tsars and emperors into the Kremlin and for church processions on Orthodox feast days. The tower was built in 1491 by the Milanese architect Pietro Antonio Solari. Until 1658 it was called

Tsar and Saviour towers

Arches and buttresses of the Saviour Tower gallery

the Florus tower, then renamed the Saviour Tower in honour of the Smolensk icon of Our Saviour which stood above the gateway. The tower has ten storeys and is decorated with white-stone carving. It is more than 67 metres high.

In 1624–1625 the Saviour Tower was one of the first in the Kremlin to have an extra tier added to it. The work was supervised by Bazhen Ogurtsov and the Englishman Christopher Galloway. At the same time Galloway installed a chiming clock on the tower, one storey lower than the present clock. The first reference to it is in 1583. Galloway's clock stopped working after a while and Peter the Great had it replaced by a new one which lasted until 1737.

The clock acquired its present appearance and musical features after a "complete reconstruction" carried out by the Butenop brothers' firm in 1851–1852. The mechanism takes up three storeys. It is set in action by three weights of 160 to 224 kilograms. Altogether the clock weighs about twenty-five

tons. The dials on each of the four sides are more than 6 metres in diameter, the hour hand is just under three metres long and the minute hand 3.28 metres.

Another carriageway tower, the Nicholas, was founded at the same time as the Saviour Tower. It was named after the icon of St Nicholas the Wonderworker painted over the gateway. The present tent spire was added in 1816–1817 in pseudo-Gothic style. After the Nicholas Tower comes the sixteen-edged corner tower by the Arsenal building. It is a powerful defensive structure with walls up to 4 metres thick. In

Cathedral of the Intercession-on-the-Moat (St Basil's). View from the Tsar Tower

Kremlin wall from the Nicholas to Saviour towers

the cellar is a spring which has survived to the present day. This tower (formerly called the Sobakina) was erected in 1492. The tent spire was added in the 17th century. It began to be called the Corner Arsenal Tower in the 18th century when the Arsenal was built nearby inside the Kremlin.

The tallest of the towers facing the Alexandrovsky Gardens is the Trinity. On the garden side it is more than 76 metres high, reaching 80 metres with the star. It was built in 1495–1499 and got its name from the nearby court of the Trinity Monastery of St Sergius

Middle Arsenal Tower

*Trinity Tower, Trinity Bridge
and Kutafia Tower*

in the Kremlin. The tent spire with Gothic arches and turrets topped by weather vanes was added in 1685. Next comes the Commandant Tower. At one time the residence of Moscow Commandant was just behind it in the Poteshny Palace. The Armoury Tower is, as one might expect, next to the Armoury.

The next tower, which has a carriageway, is the Borovitsky and got its name from the coniferous forest (bor) which once covered the southwest slope of the Kremlin hill. The road to the domestic section of the royal court passed through it: there were stables, granaries and fodder stores near Borovitsky Gate. In 1490 the tower was linked by a new brick wall with the neighbouring Sviblova Tower, which had a well and a secret passage to the river. In the first half of the 17th century pumps and reservoirs were installed here to pump water into the Kremlin. This was the city's first pumped water supply. Ever since then it

Water and Borovitsky towers

Cathedral Square →

has been called the Water Tower. In 1812 it was blown up by Napoleon's retreating army and later restored under the well-kown architect Osip Bove.

The next tower on the River Moskva side is the Annunciation, then comes the Tainitsky built by Anton Fryazin in 1485. This tower had a well and a secret exit to the river in case of siege. Next come three more towers (the First and Second Nameless Tower and the Peter Tower), which were pulled down together with the Tainitsky during Catherine the Great's reign to prepare for a new Kremlin Palace which was never built, and later restored from the original designs with minor alterations. From the defensive point of view the Beklemishev Corner Tower, named after a boyar who owned a nearby court, was particularly important.

Then comes the Constantine and Helen Tower erected in 1490 on the site of an earlier one from Dmitry Donskoy's time. The prince rode into the

Kremlin through it after the Battle of Kulikovo. The tower was named after a church which used to stand nearby.

Approaching Red Square is the stocky Tocsin Tower, whose bell used to announce fires or important events in the town. After the suppression of the "plague uprising" in 1771 the bell, which had summoned the townsfolk to revolt, was taken down and sent to Siberia. On this last stretch between the Tocsin and Saviour towers is a small tower on the wall called the Tsar Tower. It is less than 17 metres high with the weather-vane and at one time the fire-brigade bells were kept here.

Cathedral Square

The Kremlin's main square and one of the oldest in Moscow. It is ringed by some very fine monuments of mediaeval architecture. The Assumption, Annunciation and Archangel cathedrals, the Church of the Deposition of the Robe, the Ivan the Great Bell-

Tower ensemble, the Hall of Facets and the Patriarchal Palace form a unique architectural complex.

Cathedral Square has witnessed many historic events in Russian history. Official processions on important church festivals, magnificent coronation ceremonies of the Russian emperors, and receptions of foreign envoys in front of the Red Porch of the Hall of Facets all took place here. Here too funeral processions wended their way to the Archangel Cathedral, the burial place of the Moscow grand princes and tsars.

Assumption Cathedral

the semi-circular portals, windows and *zakomaras* (arched wall terminations), create an impression of austere, masculine strength.

The interior is unusually spacious, light and airy for the Middle Ages, reminiscent of a grand hall with four round pillars.

Painting covers the walls, vaults, window jambs and pillars like a rich carpet of warm red-brown tones. The fresco compositions of the 15th to 17th century form a consecutive narrative, each scene leading on to the next, full of profound content. The wall-painting has frequently been renovated and over-painted. In the 1960s it was restored to its original appearance.

From the very start the cathedral served as the burial place for the heads of the Russian Church, the metropolitans and patriarchs. The Chapel of SS Peter and Paul contains the tomb of Metropolitan Peter (d.1326) and his successor Theognostus (d.1353). Other burials are arranged round the walls. In an openwork receptacle cast in bronze by the skilled master D.Sverchkov in 1624 lie the remains of Patriarch Hermogenes who fought against the Polish invaders in the early 17th century.

The building of the main cathedral church – the centre of Russian Orthodoxy – was entrusted to the well-known Italian architect and engineer Aristotele Fioravanti. It was erected on the site of the by then very dilapidated first stone Assumption Cathedral (1326–1327) and completed in 1479.

"As if hewn from a single block" was how the chronicler describes his impression of the building, which is indeed remarkably harmonious and majestic.

The Assumption Cathedral embodied the idea of the unity of the Russian land. It also expressed the Moscow grand princes' desire to emphasise and reinforce the power of this capital of the centralised state, which was taking shape, and it symbolised the continuity and stability of sovereign rule.

The cathedral's strict proportions, powerful five domes and smooth walls, plus the serene rhythm of

Assumption Cathedral. View from the southeast. Aristotele Fioravanti. 1475–1479

Foundation of the Assumption Cathedral in Moscow. Marginal scene from the icon of "Metropolitan Peter with Scenes from his Life". Workshop of Dionysius. Early 16th cent.

Assumption Cathedral. South facade

Assumption Cathedral. Interior →

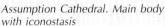

Assumption Cathedral. Main body with iconostasis

"Our Saviour of the Angry Eye". Icon. Moscow. Circa 1340s

"Dormition of the Virgin". Icon. Circa 1479

"St Ephraem the Syrian". Fresco on the sanctuary barrier of the Assumption Cathedral. Late 15th cent.

Over the centuries the cathedral has been embellished by the finest painters, jewellers, carvers and embroidresses. The very rich collection of icons from the 12th to the 17th centuries contains "St George the Warrior" (late 11th – early 12th cent.), "Our Saviour of the Golden Hair" (early 13th cent.), "Our Saviour of the Angry Eye" and a "Half-Length Christ" (both mid-14th cent.), the "Apostles Peter and Paul" and "Metropolitan Peter with Scenes from his Life"

23

Canopy with the shrine of Metropolitan Hermogenes. Moscow. D.Sverchkov. 1624. Bronze; casting, chasing

Canopy over the shrine of Metropolitan Peter. 1819

(both late 14th or early 15th cent.), the dedicational icon of the "Dormition of the Virgin" (c.1479) and many others.

One of the most famous exhibits in the Assumption Cathedral is the Throne of Ivan the Terrible, or Monomachos Throne, made in 1551. It is decorated with fine wood-carving and bas-relief compositions illustrating the political legend that the royal regalia, the cap and collar, were received from the Byzantine emperor.

Of the chandeliers note in particular the central "Harvest" candelabra said to have been made of sil-

"The Last Judgement". Fresco on the west wall of the Assumption Cathedral. 1642–1643

Tsar's throne (Throne of Monomach) in the Assumption Cathedral. Moscow. 1551

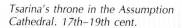

Tsarina's throne in the Assumption Cathedral. 17th–19th cent.

Metropolitan's Throne in the Assumption Cathedral. Late 15th cent.

ver confiscated by Russian soldiers from Napoleon's retreating army in 1812.

The Assumption Cathedral was not only the main church, but also an important public building. All coronations were held here from 1498 to 1896, metropolitans and patriarchs were instated and important state edicts were proclaimed.

In 1990 religious services were resumed in the cathedral. On major church feast days the service is conducted by Patriarch Alexii II of Moscow and All Russia.

Archangel Cathedral

On the southeast side of Cathedral Square, by the southern brow of Borovitsky Hill, the Italian architect Alevis Novy erected the Archangel Cathedral in 1505–1508. Like the previous cathedral on this spot, it was dedicated to the Archangel Michael, the divine protector of the Russian host. While following the traditions of Russian architecture and preserving the usual five domes, the architect gave the exterior features of Venetian Renaissance palace architecture.

The wall-painting has a long history. Ninety-two artists painted the interior between 1652 and 1666, preserving the order and composition of the 16th-century painting. Here you can see scenes about the numerous deeds of the Archangel Michael, Old Testa-

Archangel Cathedral. Alevisio Novy. 1508. View from the Ivan the Great Bell-Tower

Archangel Cathedral. Interior. Tombs by the south wall

ment scenes and a fascinating "portrait gallery" of Kievan, Vladimir and Moscow princes, symbolising the continuity and legality of royal authority.

Pride of place in the iconostasis made in 1813 belongs to the late 14th-century Russian icon of the "Archangel Michael with the Deeds of the Angels".

Until the end of the 17th century the cathedral was the burial place of the Moscow ruling dynasty It contains 45 tombs. 2 memorial slabs and two burials in shrines. The burials are under the floor and on top are brick tombs with white-stone slabs bearing foliate carved ornament and inscriptions. In 1906 the tombs were enclosed in bronze glass cases. Prince Ivan Kalita who began the unification of the Russian lands is buried here as well as Prince Dmitri Donskoy and another hero of the Battle of Kulikovo, Prince Vladimir Andreyevich. The builder of the Kremlin is buried here too, Grand Prince Ivan III. And behind the ico-

Archangel Cathedral. Interior. Tombs by the west wall. Tomb representations of the princes (frescoes on the west wall, first tier).

1652–1666. Fresco of the "Saint-Prince Alexander Nevsky" (on the left of the north face of the southwest pillar)

Archangel Cathedral. Interior. Southwest section →

Archangel Cathedral. Interior. View of the west wall from the iconostasis →

"Gideon Slaying the Midianites".
Fresco on the south wall, third tier.
1652–1666

"Archangel Michael with the Deeds
of the Angels". Icon.
Moscow. Second half of 1390s

Archangel Cathedral. Main
iconostasis. 1679–1681

nostasis lies Tsar Ivan the Terrible, next to Ivan, the
son he killed. In the main body of the cathedral is the
trellised tomb of his youngest son, Tsarevich Dmitri,
who died in Uglich in 1591, and tombs of members
of the Romanov dynasty. From Peter the Great on-
wards the Russian emperors were buried in the Peter
and Paul Cathedral in St Petersburg, with the sole ex-
ception of Peter II who died in Moscow and was buried in the Archangel Cathedral in 1730.

Annunciation Cathedral

Annunciation Cathedral. 1489–1566. View from the east

Annunciation Cathedral. North and west galleries

On the south side of Cathedral Square next to the Great Kremlin Palace is the gold-domed Annunciation Cathedral. In the second half of the 14th century where the present cathedral now stands, a small single-domed stone church was erected, later constantly rebuilt and reconstructed. In its place Grand Prince Ivan III built a small three-domed brick cathedral surrounded by a gallery on semi-basements.

Annunciation Cathedral.
North door with gold damascening.
Mid-16th cent.

The cathedral was badly damaged in the fire of 1547. In the course of restoration work during the 1560s and 1570s four chapels were erected over the corners of the galleries in the form of small single-domed churches. Another two domes were added over the main body on the west side, bringing the number of domes up to nine. At the same time the domes and roof were covered with bronze-gilt. The light, graceful proportions, rich and varied architectural forms and perfect combination of the white walls with the gold cupolas and openwork roof-edge trellis give the Annunciation Cathedral a special brilliance and elegance.

The interior is quite small. By the west wall is a wide choir gallery reached by a staircase in the wall. The cathedral's floor composed of small pieces of flint with agate and jasper is remarkably beautiful.

Annunciation Cathedral. Interior

Annunciation Cathedral. Iconostasis

The cathedral's painting contains a large number of New Testament subjects arranged in cycles, such as church feasts and Christ's Passion, miracles and parables. As well as the New Testament cycles, there are many figures of Old Testament prophets, and also apostles, bishops, martyrs, monks and warriors. The domes contain Christ Pantocrator, the Virgin of the Sign and the Lord of Sabaoth. The main place in the central body of the cathedral contains detailed illustrations of different parts of the Apocalypse. On the pillars above and below the scenes from the Apocalypse are the figures of the most revered saints, By-

zantine emperors and Russian princes who personified the idea of the continuity of power from Constantinople to Moscow. They include the Emperor Constantine and his mother Helen, Vladimir Svyatoslavich and his mother Olga, St George and St Demetrius of Salonica, the princes Boris and Gleb, Vladimir Monomach, Alexander Nevsky, Ivan Kalita and others.

The cleaning and study of the cathedral's frescoes carried out in 1977–1984 made it possible to conclude that the whole ensemble of paintings was formed at the same time, between 1547 and 1551.

"Dormition". Icon from the festival tier of the main iconostasis. First half of 15th cent.

"Virgin Mary". Icon from the Deesis tier of the main iconostasis. Last quarter of 14th cent.

"Christ Pantocrator". Icon from the Deesis tier of the main iconostasis. Last quarter of 14th cent.

"John the Baptist". Icon from the Deesis tier of the main iconostasis. Last quarter of 14th cent.

The painting in the cathedral galleries which served as a passageway into the royal palace is exceptionally interesting. It consists of a tree of Jesse composition of more than 200 figures, based on the Old Testament story of the lineage of Jesus. The tree takes up all the vaulting and a large section of the walls. The gallery frescoes contain the figures of Russian princes and ancient philosophers. Of special interest are the portraits of the "sages", Anaxagoras, Homer, Menander, Plutarch, Virgil and Plato.

The cathedral's iconostasis, which consists mainly of 14th-century and early 15th-century icons, is of great artistic value. The most outstanding work is the Deesis tier, which specialists regard as one of the fi-

nest specimens of Byzantine art of the latter half and end of the 14th century.

The six-tier iconostasis which has survived to the present day was made for the cathedral in the late 19th century. It is covered with chased and enamelled brass-gilt.

In the diaconium is a silvered brass shrine in the form of a coffin, on top of which are twenty-eight reliquaries each containing particles of sacred relics. It was made in 1894 at the factory of A.M.Postnikov.

The Annunciation Cathedral was the private church of the Russian grand princes and tsars until the Church of Our Saviour Behind-the-Golden-Trellis was built in the tsar's private apartments, and is often re-ferred to in the chronicles as being "in the grand prince's court in the vestibule". Royal weddings and christenings traditionally took place here. From the 15th century the cathedral's senior priest was the sovereign's father confessor.

The semi-basement (1360s–1416) made of large blocks of white stone has survived. The grand princes' treasury is thought to have been stored here for many years. At present it houses an exhibition entitled "The Archaeology of the Moscow Kremlin".

In recent years services have been held in the cathedral on the feast of the Annunciation which are usually conducted by the Patriarch of Moscow and All Russia, Alexii II.

Church of the Deposition of the Robe

In 1451 on the feast day of the Deposition of the Robe first introduced in Byzantium, the army of Prince Mazovshi suddenly abandoned its siege of Moscow and withdrew. To commemorate the liberation of Moscow from the Tatars the private church of the metropolitans and patriarchs erected in 1450 was dedicated to the Deposition of the Robe. After it was destroyed by fire in 1479 Pskov masters erected the present one on the site in 1484–1486 with the same name.

Church of the Deposition of the Robe. 1484–1485

Deposition of the Robe of the Holy Mother of God in Blachernae. Icon. Nazary Savin. 17th cent.

Church of the Deposition of the Robe. Iconostasis

Church of the Deposition of the Robe. West wall and vaulting

In the middle of the 17th century, when Patriarch Nikon rebuilt the Patriarchal Palace with a new private church, the Deposition of the Robe became a private church of the tsarinas and tsarevnas.

The cosy interior of this elegant single-domed church has retained its decor of the first half of the 17th century. The paintings on the walls and pillars portray Christian legends and historical events. The two upper tiers illustrate the life of the Virgin Mary, the story of her parents, childhood, youth, upbringing and the final days of her life. The two lower tiers are devoted to the Acathistos to the Virgin, a liturgical hymn of praise. The pillars bear representations of canonised Russian princes and metropolitans who are associated with important political ideas of that time. Higher up are patron saints of members of the ruling Romanov dynasty.

The icons in the Church of the Deposition were painted specially for this church and form an excellent and well preserved ensemble. One of the leading icon-painters of the first third of the seventeenth century, Nazary Istomin, painted the icons in the top three tiers and also two in the bottom tier, the "Trinity" and "Virgin with Child".

The north gallery added in the seventeenth century over the parvis contains a collection of Russian wooden sculpture of the 15th to 17th centuries: carved icons, small portable folding icons, representations of particularly revered saints, such as Nicholas of Mozhaisk, Parasceva Pyatnitsa, Florus and Laurus and St George. Note the 17th-century representation of Metropolitan Jonah carved for his tomb in the Assumption Cathedral.

41

Patriarchal Palace

Patriarchal Palace and Church of the Twelve Apostles. View from the north

Living chamber. Display of the Museum of 17th-century Russian Applied Art and Life

The three-storey Patriarchal Palace and the adjoining five-domed Church of the Twelve Apostles were the result of a rebuilding of the former Metropolitan's Court undertaken in the mid-17th century under Patriarch Nikon.

The inner chambers of the palace are connected by vestibules and passageways. The ground floor contained the domestic quarters and rooms of the patriarchal offices. The first floor consisted of ceremonial rooms and the Church of the Twelve Apostles. The patriarch's private chambers were on the second floor, and the third floor was added in the late 17th century.

The main ceremonial room is the Cross or Myrrh-Brewing Chamber. It is a large room of 280 square metres, covered by a single vault with no pillars in

Klobuk and staffs of Patriarch Nikon. Klobuk: Moscow. Mid-18th cent. Damask, satin, silk and gold thread, gold, precious stones, pearls; weaving, embroidering, enamelwork, seeds of gold. Staffs: Moscow. Second half of 17th cent. Silver; enamelwork, gilding

Church of the Twelve Apostles. Iconostasis

the middle, and intended for receptions of high church prelates and meetings of church assemblies. In 1763 the Cross Chamber acquired a stove under a carved wooden canopy for brewing myrrh, after which it became known as the Myrrh-Brewing Chamber.

In 1963 a Museum of 17th-century Russian Applied Art and Life was opened in the palace. More than a thousand exhibits illustrate the artistic tastes and customs of Russian society in that period. Here you can see various items of gold and silver plate, the work of Russian, West European and Oriental craftsmen; jewellery, rich vestments and a collection of manuscripts and early printed books, among them the "Primer" written by Karion Istomin for Peter the Great's son, Tsarevich Alexei; a collection of clocks and pocket watches; ceremonial and hunting horse

Cross Chamber. Display of the Museum of 17th-century Russian Applied Art and Life

Clock. 16th to early 17th cent. Display of the Museum of 17th-century Russian Applied Art and Life

harness; and specimens of Russian embroidery and gold cloth.

Two small rooms which have retained their media-eval architecture introduce the visitor to the 17th-century residential interior. The atmosphere is recreated with the help of a blue-and-white tiled sto-ve and various typical items of furniture: a table, a broad bench, carved high-backed chairs, a cypress-wood chest painted with a scene of falconry, a Ger-man sideboard and a Dutch cupboard, rare

*View of the Archangel Cathedral
from a Patriarchal Palace window*

specimens of foreign workmanship which appeared in the homes of the Moscow nobility at this time.

A carved portal leads into the Church of the Twelve Apostles. The iconostasis, which was brought here from the Ascension Cathedral in the Moscow Kremlin in 1929, contains a very fine collection of icons from the late 17th and early 18th centuries. On the walls is an exhibition of icons by leading Russian artists of the 18th century, such as Fyodor Rozhnov, Simon Ushakov, Fyodor Zubov, Kirill Ulanov and Ivan Saltanov.

Ivan the Great Bell-Tower ensemble. Tsar Cannon. Tsar Bell

Ivan the Great Bell-Tower ensemble. East facade

The east side of Cathedral Square contains the splendid architectural ensemble of the Ivan the Great Bell-Tower with the adjoining Assumption Belfry and Philaret Annexe. Erected in 1505–1508 by the Italian architect Bon Fryazin, the bell-tower acquired further tiers on the orders of Tsar Boris Godunov in 1600, reaching a height of 81 metres. The three rows of writing under the gold dome contain the names of Tsar Boris Godunov and his son Fyodor and the date when the new tiers were added. In the middle of the 16th century the Church of the Resurrection of Our Lord (originally the Nativity from 1555) was built onto the bell-tower, and in 1624 the ensemble acquired the Philaret Annexe with its tent roof, designed by Bazhen Ogurtsov. At the same time work began to turn the Nativity Church into a belfry. The belfry and annexe were blown up in the war of 1812 and later restored by the architect Ivan Giliardi to a design by Ivan Yegotov and Luigi Rusca.

The bell-tower and belfry contain 21 bells in all. The largest is the Assumption, which weighs about seventy tons.

Today the ground floor of the belfry is used to hold numerous exhibitions organised by the Kremlin Museums.

Tsar Cannon. Cast by Andrei Chokhov. 1586. Length 534 cm; outer diameter of barrel 120 cm; calibre 890 mm

Tsar Bell. Cast by Mikhail Motorin. 1735. Height 614 cm; diameter 660 cm

The Tsar Cannon is a remarkable piece of mediaeval artillery which testifies to the skill of the Russian armourers. It was cast in 1586 by the well-known Russian master A.Chokhov in Cannon Yard. Few armaments can rival its dimensions. The cannon has an 890 mm calibre, a barrel with an outside diameter of 1.20 metres, is 5.34 metres long and weighs 40 tons.

The cannon originally stood by the Rostrum Dais (Lobnoye mesto) in Red Square, defending the approaches to the Saviour Tower, but it was moved into the Kremlin in the 18th century. In 1856 it was placed on a gun-carriage decorated with cast patterns and four iron cannon-balls each weighing 1,000 kg were placed beside it.

At the bottom of the Ivan the Great Bell-Tower is the Tsar Bell, unrivalled both in size and artistic execution. It weighs more than 200 tons and is 6.14 metres high and 6.60 metres in diameter. The bell was cast in the Kremlin in 1735 by the master Ivan Motorin. It was still in the moulding-pit for the final touches, when the terrible fire of 1737 broke out. As a result of sudden cooling when the fire was put out some cracks appeared and a piece weighing 11.5 tons broke off.

The Tsar Bell remained in the pit for almost a hundred years, until in 1836 the architect and engineer Auguste Montferrand lifted it out and placed it on a pedestal.

Administrative building

Administrative building.
1932–1934. Architect I.I.Rerberg

Administrative building.
Pediment on south facade

Not far from the Saviour Gate is an administrative building in neo-classical style. It stands on the spot where Moscow's oldest monasteries stood until 1929, the Chudov Monastery and the Ascension convent, and also the Small Nicholas Palace. When the Soviet Government moved to Moscow in 1918 the monastery and convent were closed and in 1929 it was decided to demolish them.

The building was erected in 1932–1934 to a design by the architect I.I.Rerberg and intended for the Military School named in honour of the All-Union

*Administrative building.
Meeting hall*

*Administrative building.
Meeting hall platform*

Central Executive Committee, the first military establishment for the training of officers to be set up after the October Revolution. It stands next to Kazakov's Senate and blends in well with it in rhythm and colour. In 1938 the secretariat of the Presidium of the Supreme Soviet of the USSR was moved here. Later the interior was reconstructed to seat 1200 and used as the Kremlin Theatre until 1961.

Great Kremlin Palace

The palace was built from 1838 to 1849 (the wing with the Armoury being completed in 1851) to a design by the architect Konstantin Ton with the participation of the Moscow architects F.F.Richter, N.I.Chichagov, V.A.Bakarev and P.A.Gerasimov, the artist F.G.Solntsev and others. Emperor Nicholas I supervised the work in person, approving each page of the design for his Moscow residence.

This unique palace complex which combines the buildings of five centuries has no equivalent in Russian architecture. It consists of a system of blocks arranged in a rectangle around an inner courtyard. The facade of the main building (19th cent.) faces south, onto the River Moskva, the north side consists of the Terem Palace (17th cent.), part of the east side is formed by the Tsarina's Golden Chamber and the Hall of Facets (15th cent.), and the Imperial state apartments are on the west side.

The main facade of the palace is 125 metres long. The protruding terrace is reminiscent of an outside gallery, while the windows are adorned with surrounds of white stone and hanging "pendants", a characteristic feature of 17th-century Russian architecture.

Great Kremlin Palace during official celebrations. South facade

Great Kremlin Palace dome with bells

Great Kremlin Palace. South facade. Detail

The central part of the palace is topped by an attic with ogee-shaped kokoshniks containing representations of double-headed eagles. There is a chiming clock on the attic dome and a flag pole in the middle of the roof. Along the edge of the roof is a patterned gilded trellis.

The new building materials, metal constructions and engineering techniques used in the construction of the Great Kremlin Palace became models for 19th-century Russian architects and were used very widely.

In size and magnificence the Great Kremlin Palace excelled all other buildings of its day.

In 1932–1934 the splendid St Andrew and St Alexander halls of the former imperial residence were combined to form an austere conference hall (architect I.A.Ivanov Shitz), where Communist party conferences and sessions of the Supreme Soviets of the USSR and RSFSR were held. In 1999 the halls were restored to their original splendour.

Today the Great Kremlin Palace is used for holding official receptions by the President of the Russian Federation, top-level negotiations and the signing of major international treaties.

Hall of Facets

The year 1480, when the army of Grand Prince Ivan III of Moscow forced the Golden Horde invaders to retreat, marked the liberation of Russia from Mongol-Tatar overlordship. To enhance the prestige of the young state a grandiose building programme began in Moscow with the assistance of the finest Russian and foreign masters.

Ivan III invited the Italian architects Alevisio Fryazin, Marco Fryazin and Pietro Antonio Solari to erect a large and sumptuous palace, which was constructed between 1487 and 1508 and subsequently frequently rebuilt. Only the official throne room of this old palace has survived, the Hall of Facets. Its main facade, which looks onto Cathedral Square, is faced with blocks of four-faceted white stone, which explains the name.

Hall of Facets. Main facade.
Architects Marco Fryazin, Pietro
Antonio Solari. 1487–1491

Hall of Facets and the Red Porch.
View from the southest

*Hall of Facets. Sacred Vestibule.
Interior*

This majestic building, square in plan, stands on a high semi-basement. The main body consists of a huge, single-pillared hall covering an area of 495 square metres. The interior is both sumptuous and austere. The cross vaulting rests in the middle on a massive four-sided pillar, richly decorated with white-stone carving and gilt.

The decor of the Hall of Facets has frequently been renovated and changed. In the second half of the 16th century the walls were painted with ecclesiastical-Biblical compositions. After several fires in 1672 the tsar commissioned the icon-painter Simon Ushakov to compile a detailed and accurate inventory of the original subjects and texts. At the end of the 17th century the paintings were whitewashed over and the walls hung with scarlet cloth, which by the middle of the 19th century had been replaced by red velvet with silver applique double-headed eagles. For the coronation of Emperor Alexander III (1883) the walls of the Hall of Facets were again painted by icon-painters from the village of Palekh, the Belousov brothers, who adhered closely to the old inventory.

The choice of subjects in the painting was determined by the main aim, to extol centralised power and affirm its continuity. Hence the compositions showing the twenty-four members of the princely dynasty of Rurikoviches, including Grand Prince Vladimir of Kiev with his twelve sons whom he is instructing how to live righteously and rule wisely. It is easy to see the parallels between the Old Testament subjects and events in Russian history. For example, the future ruler Boris Godunov is portrayed

*Chandelier in the Hall of Facets.
Mid-19th cent.*

Hall of Facets. Interior

next to Tsar Theodore, son of Ivan the Terrible, while opposite is a detailed and colourful illustration of the parable about Joseph the Beautiful.

For a long time the Hall of Facets was the largest ceremonial hall in Moscow. It was used to receive ambassadors and celebrate important state occasions. The Council of Boyars also met here. During official dinners the hall was spread with carpets and the tables laid with gold and silver plate. Ceremonial thrones from the Armoury were brought in here.

54

Study of Patriarch Aleksii II in the semi-basement of the Hall of Facets

The entrance to the Hall of Facets was from Cathedral Square through the Red Porch and adjoining Sacred Vestibule, the name of which is explained by the paintings illustrating the Holy Scriptures which adorned its walls.

In the 1990s the rooms in the semi-basement of the Hall of Facets were transferred to the Moscow Patriarchate. They now form the Patriarch's Kremlin residence.

Tsarina's Golden Chamber.
Interior

Tsarina's Golden Chamber.
White-stone portal. 16th cent.

The reception halls of the tsarinas, the Tsarina's Golden Chamber, is first mentioned under 1526. There is also a reference to the fact that in 1589 during the reign of Tsar Theodore his wife, Irina Godunova, received Russian and foreign church dignitaries here. It was then that the walls were painted on a background of gold, which gave the chamber its name.

The paintings that exist today date back to the early 17th century. Over the centuries they were frequently overpainted in oil paint. And not until the 1970s, after nine years of painstaking work, did the restorers succeed in removing the later layers.

The main theme of the compositions is the triumph of the Christian faith. This idea determined the choice of figures to be represented. An important place is occupied by detailed legends about Princess Olga, who was the first member of the princely family to adopt Christianity and did much to establish the Christian faith in Russia. Princess Olga is shown as heir to the ancient centres of Christianity, Rome and Constantinople.

In the Tsarina's Golden Chamber the Russian tsarinas received congratulations on church and family feasts. It was also used for wedding ceremonies, funeral banquets for tsarinas who had passed away, and receiving high-ranking guests.

In the 17th century the churches of Our Saviour Not Made With Hands (1635) and the Crucifixion (1681) which stood on the vaulting of the Tsarina's Golden Chamber required more support, so the vaults were reinforced with cross arches and additional iron braces, which altered the interior considerably.

Tsarina's Golden Chamber.
Representation of the Saint-Tsarina
Irina. South vault

Tsarina's Golden Chamber.
Northwest side

Terem Palace

Erected on the orders of Tsar Mikhail Romansov in 1635–1636 by the Russian builders Bazhen Ogurtsov, Antip Konstantinov, Trefil Sharutin and Larion Ushakov. The lowest storey consists of the 15th-century semi-basement which is a continuation of the semi-basement of the Hall of Facets. From the Sacred Vestibule you could get to Boyars' Landing, a terrace on the vaulted roof of the semi-basement. From there an open staircase led up to the vaulted roof of the 16th-century Workshop Chambers, where the two residential storeys of the Terem Palace were erected, set back somewhat from the edge of the walls. From the gallery over the Workshop Chambers, which was called the Upper Saviour Landing, you passed through the splendid Golden Porch up to the next floor, the tsar's apartments. The top floor or Gold Roofed Teremok, is surrounded by a gallery with a pointed watchtower on the west side. This is topped by a high saddleback roof with a metal ridge trellis and weather-vanes. The unusual, exotic appearance of the Terem Palace delighted contemporaries, who admired these "most wondrous chambers".

Terem Palace. 1635–1636. Architects Bazhen Ogurtsov, Antip Konstantinov, Trefil Sharutin, Larion Ushakov. North facade

Terem Palace. Pediment and window surround of the Throne Room

Terem Palace. White-stone decor

The portals, windows surrounds and cornices of the Terem Palace are covered with fine white-stone carving. It consists of ornamental braiding, a geometrical pattern, fantastic animals and birds, and heraldic double-headed eagles. The paired windows of the upper storeys are adorned with fine arches and typical 17th-century hanging pendants. At one time the rich carving was combined with polychrome painting: examination of the portals and window surrounds has revealed traces of ochre, vermilion and

Golden Trellis. 1670. Iron; forging, carving, gilding

Golden Trellis doors

Terem Palace. Throne Room

*Tiled stove in the Throne Room.
Mid-19th cent. reconstruction*

light-green paint and gilding. The rich carving is enhanced by the tiled friezes on the two upper storeys.

A multitude of staircases and passageways linked the palace with Boyars' Landing, the ceremonial Hall of Facets, the Tsarina's Golden Chamber, and the palace churches. In the second half of the 17th century the staircase that led to the Terem Palace from Boyars' Landing and the Upper Saviour Church that stands opposite were decorated with a painted and gilded cast-iron trellis. The pattern of interlaced spirals and strange creatures is most inventive.

When the Great Kremlin Palace was built in the nineteenth century, part of Boyars Landing was roofed over with high vaulting and turned into the St Vladimir Hall. The Upper Saviour Landing and Golden Porch were also roofed over and altered: at the bottom of the porch two white-stone lions made in 1845 bear shields with the monogram of Emperor Nicholas I, in whose reign these alterations were made. The arches of the porch are adorned with hanging pendants in the form of lion masks. In their mouths the lions are holding the so-called "apple of silence", to show that the tsar's residence guarded by them would not divulge its secrets.

Terem Palace.
Inside passageway

Portal of the Golden-Roofed
Teremok

The royal apartments in the Terem Palace with their vaulted ceilings and wooden floors are arranged one after the other. The windows in each room have coloured glass and wide wooden sills covered with intricate carving. The first room is the Ante-Chamber where the boyars and state secretaries used to wait for the tsar. The second is called the Duma or Assembly room, where the Tsar and his boyars decided affairs of state. The third room is the Throne Room or Cabinet. The painting in goldenish-red tones, the coats-of-arms of the different Russian regions and state double-headed eagles, and the ornament on the round tiled stove make the interior of this room particularly impressive. The middle window is marked on

Gold-Roofed Teremok. Interior

*View of the Terem church domes
from the Gold-Roofed Teremok*

the outside by carved round columns resting on sculptures of lions. The last room in the royal apartments is the Bedchamber which has a carved wooden bed with a canopy and a small Oratory with a carved iconostasis containing icons of the seventeenth and eighteenth centuries.

The interior decor and original wall-painting of the Terem Palace have not survived. The painting you see today was executed in 1836 by the artist T.Kiselev from designs by Academician F.G.Solntsev. The tiled stoves and few pieces of furniture were made under the supervision of F.F.Richter from seventeenth-century models.

Palace churches

Domes of the Assumption Cathedral,
Ivan the Great Bell-tower and Terem
churches

*Church of the Resurrection
of Lazarus. 1393–1394*

In the seventeenth century there were eleven churches in the royal palace, not counting the many chapels and oratories. Today there are six.

In 1393–1394 the Church of the Nativity of the Virgin was built on the orders of Dmitry Donskoy's widow, Princess Yevdokia. It was the grand princesses' private church. In 1514 the Italian architect Alevisio Novy made use of the old building by turning it into the semi-basement of the new church built on top of it. The old chapel was reconsecrated as the Church of the Resurrection of Lazarus, which is now one of the oldest architectural monuments in the Kremlin. The Church of the Nativity of the Virgin acquired its present appearance after rebuilding in 1681–1684, and the wall painting was executed in oil paints under the supervision of T.Kiselev in the middle of the nineteenth century. The church's gilded dome can be seen on the west side of the Terem Palace roof.

Church of the Nativity of the Virgin.
Iconostasis. 18th–19th cent.

Upper Saviour Cathedral.
Iconostasis. 18th–19th cent.
Icons 1670s

At the same time as the Terem Palace the same masters built the Upper Saviour Cathedral with the Chapel of St John the Baptist (originally St John of Belgorod), the private church of the Russian tsars. The present baroque iconostasis, adorned with carving and gilt, dates back to the eighteenth century. The four chased icon-panels and the Royal Doors of niel-loed silver were made in the late eighteenth and early nineteenth centuries. The collection of icons includes works by the finest royal artists in the second half of the 17th century.

The Church of St Catherine, built in brick by the Englishman John Taylor in 1627, stands in the Terem Palace. In 1847 its interior was redecorated to a design by D.N.Chichagov. The iconostasis was designed by F.G.Solntsev. In 1654 the Church of St Eudoxia was erected over St Catherine's and rededicated in

Church of the Nativity of the Virgin.
Refectory. Interior

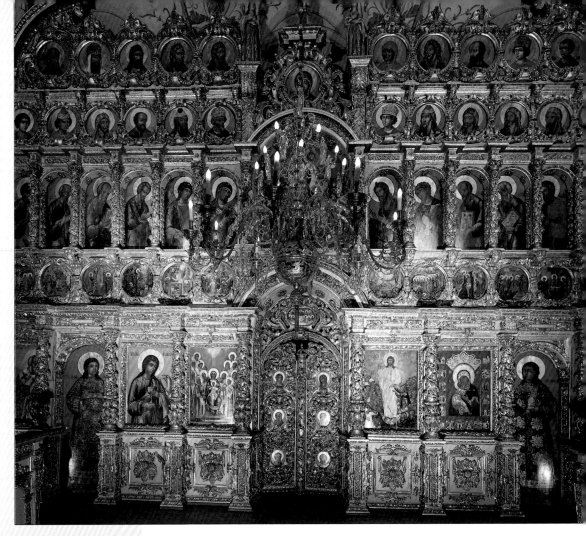

*Resurrection of Christ
(Slovushchego). Iconostasis. 1678–
1679*

1681 to the Resurrection of Christ (later the Resurrection Slovushchego). The church's main decoration is its multichrome iconostasis of 1678 with icons of the same period and a carved and gilded choir gallery. The colours of the iconostasis are most unusual: a combination of the smooth turquoise-blue background with open-work carved gilded and silvered details covered with coloured lacquer. The Church of the Crucifixion (Elevation of the Cross of Our Lord) was erected over the Upper Saviour Cathedral at the request of Tsar Fyodor Alexeyevich. Its iconostasis was the work of Vasily Poznansky and is unique in Russian art: only the faces and hands of the saints are painted in oils, the robes and background being made of pasted applique precious textiles.

In 1683 the four private churches, the Upper Saviour, Resurrection, Crucifixion and St Catherine's, were joined under a single roof, which has eleven domes with open-work gilt crosses that look splendid from Cathedral Square.

*Resurrection of Christ
(Slovushchego). Royal Doors*

Church of the Crucifixion. Iconostasis, 19th cent. Icons, 1682

Church of the Crucifixion. "Our Saviour in a Crown of Thorns". Icon. Vasily Poznansky. 1682

Church of St Catherine the Martyr. Iconostasis. 1844–1846

Halls of Orders

St George Hall. Doors from the St Vladimir Hall

The five halls of Orders in the Great Kremlin Palace form the only ensemble of its kind in Russian architecture. They embody the idea of eternal remembrance of the many generations of people who served their homeland and were decorated with its highest awards.

The largest ceremonial hall, St George's, is dedicated to Russia's military award, the Order of St George

St George Hall. Doors with the St George Cross on the glass. Detail

St George Hall. Interior

instituted in 1769 by Empress Catherine the Great. The hall was conceived as a temple of glory to Russian arms. The solemn and majestic white of the walls and vaulting with a relief pattern is enhanced by the shimmering of the rich gilt chandeliers, lamp brackets, and the ornamental gilt carving on the doors. The memorial plaques that cover the walls and pylons are inscribed in gold with the names of the regiments and individuals awarded the Order of St

George. Along the walls are eighteen spiral columns crowned with marble statues by I.P.Vitali. They are allegorical figures with shields bearing the coat-of-arms of the various regions that made up Russia from the fifteenth to nineteenth centuries.

The St Vladimir Hall is dedicated to the Order of St Vladimir instituted in 1782 by Empress Catherine the Great. The walls are faced with white and pink

St Vladimir Hall. Interior

St Catherine Hall. Interior

St Alexander Hall. Interior →

St Andrew Hall. Interior →

artificial marble and designed in the shape of arches. They support a tent-shaped vault with an octagonal dome and a bronze-gilt chandelier. The vault and cornices have gilded moulding. Round medallions contain the St Vladimir cross with the motto: "Benefit, Honour and Glory". An interesting feature of the hall's planning is that it unites a number of buildings from different periods: the doors and staircases on the various sides lead to the 15th-century Hall of Facets,

the 16th-century Tsarina's Golden Chamber, the 17th-century Terem Palace and the 19th-century St George's Hall.

The St Catherine Hall, the Empress's Throne Room, is dedicated to the Order of St Catherine instituted by Peter the Great in 1714. The order's cross on a ribbon with the motto "For Love and the Fatherland" adorns the carved, gilt doors and the walls hung with grey silk.

Great Kremlin Palace guest annexe.
Antechamber

The St Alexander Hall is named in honour of the Order of St Alexander Nevsky instituted in 1725. The order's motto is "For Labour and the Fatherland". The walls are faced with pink artificial marble and the spherical dome is adorned with double-headed eagles and the order's cross, as well as the coats-of-arms of the Russian gubernias and regions.

The St Andrew Throne Room of the Russian emperors is dedicated to the Order of St Andrew the First-Called instituted by Peter the Great in 1698. The walls are hung with pale blue silk, the colour of the order's ribbon, and decorated with its cross.

At the same time as the Alexander and Andrew halls were restored (in 1999) work was carried out to reconstruct the adjacent gallery and the buildings added to the palace in the 1930s. The author of the project and artistic director of the reconstruction was I.S.Glazunov and his workshop. The new halls, the Petrovsky, Shtofny, Green and Red, are intended for official events.

Great Kremlin Palace guest annexe.   *Great Kremlin Palace guest annexe.*
Petrovsky Hall   *Shtofny Hall*

75

The St Catherine Hall is adjoined on the north by three rooms, the State (Green) Drawing Room, the State Bedchamber and the State Dressing Room, which contain a remarkable collection of Russian decorative and applied art of the nineteenth century. The porcelain for them was supplied exclusively by the Imperial Porcelain Works in St Petersburg, the furniture mainly by the Petersburg workshops of P.Gambs and A. and K.Tour, and the textiles for the upholstery, curtains and wall hangings by the G.G.Sapozhnikov Moscow factory.

The State Drawing Room is a spacious room with a vaulted ceiling painted by the Italian artist Giuseppe Artari. The walls are hung with green and gold cloth, and the doors and tables are inlaid with bronze, tortoiseshell, mother-of-pearl and precious types of

Chair from the Red Drawing Room

wood in the Boulle style. There are also articles of bronze and porcelain, of which the most noteworthy is the candelabra in "Japanese" style with sixty-six candle-holders and vases for real flowers.

The main decoration of the State Bedchamber or Red Drawing Room are the columns of monolithic greenish-grey Italian marble and the fireplace of jasper made in the Urals.

The walls of the State Dressing Room are faced with walnut panels carefully fitted together without a single nail or glue by the master Karl Herts. The form of the alabaster chandelier made in the 1840s in the Moscow workshop of Santino Campioni was inspired by classical models.

The Imperial Apartments

*Imperial Apartments.
Empress's Drawing Room*

The ground floor of the Great Kremlin Palace contains the private apartments of the Imperial family. The suites of rooms run along the main and west facades of the palace and consist of seven residential rooms and four small chambers used for guard duty and receiving courtiers.

In the interiors the architects and designers made use of many styles, such as the devices and decorative elements of baroque, rococo and classicism. Each room is different and a perfect artistic whole.

Imperial Apartments.
Empress's Study

Imperial Apartments.
Empress's Study. Clock. France.
First half of 19th cent.

Imperial Apartments.
Mirror in the Imperial Dining Room

Massive pillars divide the apartments into two parts: a long corridor and the living area of the room with elegant carving and gilding, exquisite wall hangings, magnificent furniture and beautiful fireplaces.

The rooms in the imperial apartments are lit by cone-shaped chandeliers of bronze-gilt with multi-tiered garlands of crystal pendants. The floors are covered with carefully selected patterned carpets. The doors are made of various types of wood and richly decorated with inlay and relief wood-carving.

The suite begins with the Dining Room. Its decor is based on classical principles and antique motifs: a combination of the light tones of the artificial marble on the walls, the white marble statures of Hymenaeus and Leda, and the crater-shaped vases showing Olympic gods, maenads and satyrs.

In the decor of the Drawing (Empress's Reception) Room one can sense the whimsical elegance of baroque: the delicate pastel tones of white, pink and blue with gold in the flower painting and the curves of the gilt furniture. There is a large chandelier decorated with masses of porcelain flowers made at the Imperial Porcelain Works. The two pineapples, one at the top and the other at the bottom, explain its name – the Pineapple chandelier.

The Empress's Study is one of the most tastefully decorated rooms in the palace. The white and coloured marble, gilding, bronze, mirrors and rich crimson upholstery and wall hangings harmonise perfectly with the Boulle furniture. The Empress's study is connected to her boudoir by a room in which her ladies-in-waiting used to be on duty. The walls are panelled in walnut and have decorative painting on a crimson background. There is an interesting vase of white marble in the form of the Three Graces holding a basket of flowers.

The Empress's Boudoir is decorated in silvery pink tones. The wall hangings, upholstery and window drapings are of the same material. The fireplace is faced with malachite. It looks as if it has been hewn out of a single slab of this remarkable stone, so carefully were the small pieces of malachite selected for colour and pattern by the craftsmen at the Yekaterinburg polishing and cutting factory. The bronze clock on the mantelpiece has an enamel dial with a calendar showing the months, days and phases of the moon.

The blue colour scheme of the former Bedchamber was intended to resemble the clear night sky. The splendid fireplace of white Carrara marble is adorned with a fine clock. The bedchamber is separated from the Emperor's Study by a small room which is panelled with ashwood and has green wall hangings.

Imperial Apartments.
Empress's Boudoir

Imperial Apartments.
Empress's Boudoir. Clock.
France. First half of 19th cent.

Imperial Apartments.
Emperor's Study

Imperial Apartments.
Bedchamber

The Emperor's Study has an austere, official appearance. The walls are panelled with light ashwood and the furniture is made of Karelian birchwood with black leather upholstery.

The furniture in the Emperor's Reception Room is upholstered in velvet with a pile that changes its pattern according to the lighting and was made at the G.G.Sapozhnikov factory in Moscow.

Today all these rooms are carefully preserved and only rarely used during receptions for high-ranking foreign guests.

Poteshny Palace. The State Kremlin Palace

The Poteshny Palace stands between the Trinity and Commandant towers and is the only surviving specimen of a boyar's palace in the Kremlin. It was built in 1652 for the boyar I.D.Miloslavsky. Later it went to the crown and was connected by a passageway with the royal palace. From 1672 to 1676 theatrical performances ("potekhi") were put on here, which explains its name. In 1679 it was used as living quarters for members of the royal family and extended. At the end of the seventeenth century it housed the Police Department, and in 1806 I.V.Yegotov rebuilt it as the living quarters and chancellery of the commandant of Moscow, adding pseudo-gothic details. In 1874–1875 N.A.Shokhin tried to restore its original appearance during repair work.

The last major building in the Kremlin is the State Kremlin Palace built in 1959–1961 by the Trinity Gate on the site of the old Armoury and a number of auxiliary blocks. Rectangular in plan, it contains more than 800 different rooms, is 29 metres high and goes 15 metres underground. The conference hall can seat 6,000. The palace was intended for Communist Party congresses, international events and official meetings. Today the State Kremlin Palace is used mainly for concerts and also for opera and ballet productions.

Poteshny Palace. 1651. View from the southeast

State Kremlin Palace. 1960–1961. Architects M.V.Posokhin, A.A.Mdoyants and others

The Armoury

The Armoury is Russia's oldest museum, a treasury of world-wide importance, containing precious objects from nine centuries. Its various collections reflect the main stages in the development of the Russian state and the history of Russian and foreign culture.

Over the more than five centuries since it was founded the Armoury's functions have changed from time to time: apart from looking after the royal regalia, it also supervised the activities of a large number of different workshops, where talented masters were commissioned by the sovereign or high church digni-

Armoury building. K.A.Ton. 1851

Armoury. Grand Staircase

Room 1. Russian gold and silverware (12th to 17th cent.)

Chain, neck pendant and two bracelets from the Sudzha trove. North Black Sea Coast. 4th to 5th cent. Gold, glass; casting

taries to make various liturgical items, including cases for gospels and icons, chalices, crosses, censers and panagias (pectoral icons worn by metropolitans and patriarchs), and also rich tableware for the court, such as plates, bowls, loving-cups and goblets. These objects testify to the fertile imagination and remarkable skill of their makers. They all bear the stamp of a special national quality.

In early times the Armoury did not consist of exhibition halls with glass cases and display platforms as it does today. The riches there were demonstrated far

Chalice. Russia. Ryazan. 12th cent. Silver; chasing, carving, gilding

Ryazan trove. Russia. Ryazan. 12th cent. Gold, precious stones, pearls; cloisonné enamelwork, filigree, seeds of gold

more effectively by written records penned by Armoury scribes, their descriptions of how the tsar was dressed during a ceremonial procession, which crown he wore, and which particular rod he chose to receive foreign envoys. The admiration expressed by foreigners in their reports of regalia, gold and silver plate and gem-studded ceremonial weapons is similar to the reaction of visitors to the Armoury today. Whereas in former times embassies were met to the accompaniment of clinking silver chains by richly attired horsemen on steeds in magnificent harness, today high-ranking guests are invited to admire that very same harness in the Armoury display.

The museum is housed in a building specially erected for it in 1851 to a design by the architect Konstantin Ton. It has nine display rooms, four on the ground floor and five on the first.

Room 1 contains a small but very valuable collection of Byzantine art from the 4th to 15th centuries. Of special interest are the items from a treasure trove discovered in 1927 in the upper reaches of the River Sudzha. They are pieces of jewellery dating back to

Small Zion. Moscow. 1486. Copper; chasing, gilding, filigree

Gospel. Moscow. Early 15th cent. Gold, precious stones; chasing, filigree

the 4th and 5th centuries: a chain, a neck pendant and two bracelets and a silver-gilt jug bearing the nine muses.

The unique pieces of jewellery from the pre-Mongol period include objects found in 1822 on the site of Old Ryazan. They are beautifully made in cloisonne enamel and have all sorts of intricate filigree patterns.

The silver chalice made in the 1220s or 1230s is a valuable specimen of Vladimir-Suzdalian workmanship. Its perfect proportions, smooth lines and deliberately simple, fine ornament are most appropriate for a vessel used in the sacrament of Holy Communion.

*Censer. Moscow Kremlin
Workshops. 1598. Gold, precious
stones; chasing, niello. A gift from
Irina Godunova to the Archangel
Cathedral of the Moscow Kremlin*

*Gospel. Moscow. First half of 17th
cent. G.Ovdokimov. 1632. Gold,
precious stones, pearls; chasing,
enamelwork*

Two windows in Room one contain articles by
15th-century Moscow craftsmen. The Morozov Gospel is a rare item for this period. It is thought to have
been commissioned by Metropolitan Photius for the
Assumption Cathedral in the Moscow Kremlin.

In the 16th century Moscow became the leading
centre for gold and silverware. Note in particular the
set of liturgical objects consisting of a censer, chalice, paten with a "star" top and two plates made in
1598 for Tsarina Irina Godunova as a donation to
the Archangel Cathedral in the Moscow Kremlin. The
censer in the form of a single-domed church is particular sumptuous. It is decorated with precious stones
and nielloed figures of apostles and saints with the
same names as members of the Tsar's family.

Room 2. Russian gold and silver-ware (17th to early 20th cent.)

Dipper (kovsh). Belonged to Tsar Michael Romanov. Moscow Kremlin Workshops. 1618. Gold, precious stones, pearls; forging, niello

Gospel. Moscow Kremlin Workshops. 1571. Gold, precious stones, pearls; chasing, enamelwork, filigree, seeds of gold, niello. A gift from Ivan the Terrible to the Annunciation Cathedral of the Moscow Kremlin

Loving cup (bratina). Moscow Kremlin Workshops. First half of 17th cent. Gold, precious stones, pearls; niello

Yendova. Moscow. 1644. Silver; chasing, carving, gilding

The 16th century saw the rebirth of enamelwork. A fine specimen is the 1554 case for the measurement icon of Ivan the Terrible's first son, Ivan. Note also the rich gold case for the 1571 Gospel manuscript, a gift by Ivan the Terrible to the Kremlin's Annunciation Cathedral. The case is adorned with a filigree pattern coloured with delicate shades of enamelwork.

The Armoury possesses the fullest collection of articles by 17th-century Russian masters. The gold and silverware decorated with precious stones and pearls, such as dippers, loving-cups, wine-cups and *korchiks* (small dippers), conjure up vivid pictures of court life during that period.

Presentational dipper. Moscow. 1755. Silver; casting, chasing, gilding

Chalice. Moscow. 1789. K.Muller. Gold, diamonds; casting, chasing, enamelwork, filigree

In the late 17th and early 18th centuries Russian and West European culture drew closer as a result of Peter the Great's reforms, and the subsequent development of Russian art proceeded along more or less the same lines as in Western Europe. The traditional forms of drinking vessels changed, as did their function. Thus, for example, the mediaeval "boat-shaped" dippers lost the function of a drinking vessel and began to be used exclusively as presentation awards or simply as presents.

The 19th century brought changes in the organisation of jewellery making. Associations appeared in Moscow and St Petersburg, the most famous being the firms of Carl Faberge, P.Sazikov, and I.Khlebnikov and the factories of P.Ovchinnikov and V.Semyonov. The House of Faberge became world-famous. It produced, inter alia, figurines made of semi-precious stones, snuff-boxes, powder-boxes and items of

"Moscow Kremlin" egg. St Petersburg, C.Faberge firm. 1913. H.Wigstrom, miniaturist V.Zuyev. Gold, silver, onyx; casting, enamelwork, carving

"Romanov Tercentenary" egg. St Petersburg, C.Faberge firm. 1913. H.Wigstrom, miniaturist V.Zuyev. Gold, diamonds, purpurine; casting, chasing, enamelwork

Egg with portraits of Nicholas II's children (and model of Alexandrovsky palace inside). St Petersburg, C.Faberge firm. 1908. H.Wigstrom. Gold, silver, diamonds, rubies, nephrite; casting, enamelwork, chasing, watercolour

jewellery. It was distinguished from other jewellers of the period by its beautifully made "Easter eggs with a surprise". For eleven years the firm received orders from the Imperial court for these eggs.

Room 3. Window with a collection of Iranian arms (16th to 17th cent.)

Room 3. Oriental and European ceremonial arms (15th–19th cent.)

The arms and armour of the 12th to 19th centuries bear witness to some great historic events. The Armoury was the court treasury. This explains why all the specimens of Russian, West Europe and Oriental military, ceremonial and hunting firearms are richly decorated with all types of artistic metal-working and inlaid with precious stones, mother-of-pearl and ivory.

The Armoury possesses a collection of armour, cold steel and firearms dating from the 15th to 19th centuries. Particularly noteworthy are the full sets of ceremonial armour for rider and horse made by Kunz Lochner, a Nuremberg craftsman. This suit of armour was a present to Tsar Fyodor Ivanovich from King Stefan Bathory of Poland in 1584.

The collection of Oriental arms consists mainly of items by Iranian and Turkish craftsmen of the 16th and 17th centuries, such as daggers, sabres, shields, quiver and bow cases (saadaks) and helmets. The 16th-century shield of Iranian workmanship which belonged to F.I.Mstislavsky is remarkable for its fine artistic qualities.

Room 4. Part of the display
of Russian arms ↑

Room 4. Part of the display
of Russian arms
←

The most important part of the arms and armour section is the collection of Russian arms of the 12th to 17th centuries. It contains a helmet of the late 12th or early 13th century that belonged to Prince Yaroslav, son of Vsevolod and father of Alexander Nevsky, a ceremonial helmet of Tsar Michael Romanov made by the talented master Nikita Davydov, Tsar Boris Godunov's famous shirts of mail, Prince Dmitri Pozharsky's sabre, and various Russian military decorations and orders. Most of the items were made by craftsmen in the Armoury of the Moscow Kremlin.

An important place in the collection belongs to arms produced in the 18th and 19th centuries in such centres as Tula, St Petersburg, Sestroretsk, Olonets and Zlatoust.

Also on display in this room are Swedish arms and ammunition, trophies from the Battle of Poltava in 1709, which include King Charles XII of Sweden's hunting set.

The Armoury has one of the world's richest collections of 13th- to 19th-century silverware from England, Holland, Denmark, Poland, Sweden, Germany and France.

The nucleus of the collection consists of diplomatic and commercial gifts to Russian rulers which illustrate most vividly the history of Russia's political and trading relations and the growth of its international prestige. To stress the importance of an ambassadorial mission, European and Oriental monarchs used to send Russian rulers pieces of the most valuable and fashionable silverware and articles made of natural rare materials and precious stones executed by the finest craftsmen. The tsar could refuse to accept the

gifts if he felt that they were not in keeping with his rank, as was the case when money was offered rather than artistic objects. The etiquette of those days allowed superiors to give money to their inferiors, but not the reverse.

Pride of place belongs to the English silver of the second half of the sixteenth to the mid-seventeenth century. No other museum in the world has such a rich and varied collection. In England itself articles of silver were melted down during the Civil War of 1642 to 1649 for coinage. During the revolution of 1917 the Armoury collections were in danger, as were all the imperial valuables evacuated during the First World War from the areas of military operations

Room 5. West European silver
(13th–19th cent.)

Horn of Plenty Goblet. Hamburg.
17th cent. D.Thor Moye. Silver:
chasing, casting, engraving, gilding

Melon Goblet. Hamburg.
1631–1633. G.Lambrecht II. Silver;
casting, chasing, gilding

Leopard. London, England. 1600–
1601. Silver; casting, gilding

Heavenly Globe. Hamburg. 17th
cent. G.Lambrecht II. Silver; casting, chasing, engraving, gilding

Goblet. Hamburg. 1598. J. Mores
the Elder. Silver; casting, chasing,
gilding

Goblet. Emden (Germany). 1612.
Coconut shell, silver; casting,
chasing, gilding, coconut shell
carving

Goblet. Germany. 17th cent. Ivory,
silver; casting, chasing, engraving,
gilding, ivory carving

Washing set. Augsburg. 17th cent.
J.H.Mannlich. Mountain crystal,
silver, precious stones; enamelwork

and from Petrograd for safekeeping in the Moscow Kremlin. All the gold and diamonds of the Hermitage and Petrograd's many museums and surrounding palaces lay in sealed crates in the Armoury, cellars and corridors of the Great Kremlin Palace. In the few days of October-November 1917 when there was fighting in Moscow and the Kremlin was surrounded and bombarded with artillery, the keepers at the Armoury did not leave their posts and guarded the valuables in their care for future generations.

The superb collection of Dutch seventeenth-century silver contains about 140 items by craftsmen in Amsterdam, the Hague, Utrecht and Leyden. They are articles that were intended as presents for the Russian tsar and a large group specially commissioned by the merchant Grigory Stroganov.

Cup and wash-bowl. Cup –
Augsburg. First half of 17th cent.
Mother of pearl, silver; casting,
chasing, gilding. Wash-bowl –
Antwerp. 1540s – 1560s. Mother-
of-pearl shells, silver, pearls,
precious stones; casting, chasing,
gilding

Olympic service. Sevres. Early 19th
cent. Porcelain; painting, gilding

The most important ambassadorial collection of silver consists of gifts from Sweden in the seventeenth century, the period when Russo-Swedish diplomatic relations were most intensive. Most of them were presented between 1647 and 1699 by embassies from Queen Christina, Charles X, Charles XI and Charles XII. They were fashioned mainly by German masters in Nuremberg, Augsburg and Hamburg, towns where the art of the silversmiths had been passed down from father to son for many generations. The display also includes ambassadorial gifts from Poland and Denmark.

The windows in the display contain sideboards like the ones on which the silver of the Russian sovereigns used to impress and amaze foreign guests.

Room 6. Precious textiles, ecclesiastical and ornamental embroidery (14th to 18th cent.). Secular dress in Russia (16th to early 20th cent.)

Saccos and staff of Metropolitan Peter. Russia. 1322. Saccos: gold satin – Byzantium, late 13th cent.; decorative embroidery – Russia, 14th cent.; plates – Russia, 15th to 17th cent. Satin, gold and silver thread, pearls; embossing, embroidery, chasing, gilding. Staff: Russia, 14th cent., renovated in Moscow, 1677. Wood, silver, metal; carving, casting, gilding

The Armoury has a very rich collection of valuable textiles, embroidery and dress. Its value lies in the fact that the textiles from Byzantium (14th–15th cent.), Turkey and Iran (16th–17th cent.), Western Europe (16th–18th cent.) and Russia (17th–19th cent.) are not individual fragments, but well-preserved complete works, such as secular and ecclesiastical dress, table-cloths, curtains, horse-cloths, etc., which adds greatly to the cultural and social importance of the collection.

The items of Russian ecclesiastical and ornamental embroidery of the fourteenth to seventeenth centuries are very fine. They include palls, podeas, aers and coffin cloths embroidered with coloured silks, gold and silver thread and pearls, fine specimens of "needle painting". The earliest item of ornamental embroidery is on the saccos (1322) of Metropolitan Peter.

The collection of secular dress from the 16th to 19th centuries is also of great historical and artistic interest. It includes Metropolitan Philip's winter coat of 16th-century homespun cloth, items of clothing of the Russian tsars and emperor and the coronation dresses of the Russian empresses from Catherine I to Alexandra Fydorovna (Nicholas II's wife) designed according to the dictates of European fashion at that time.

Coronation dress of Catherine the Great. Russia. 1762. Brocade, decorative embroidery on applique, lace

Coronation uniform of Emperor Nicholas II and coronation dress of Empress Alexandra Fyodorovna

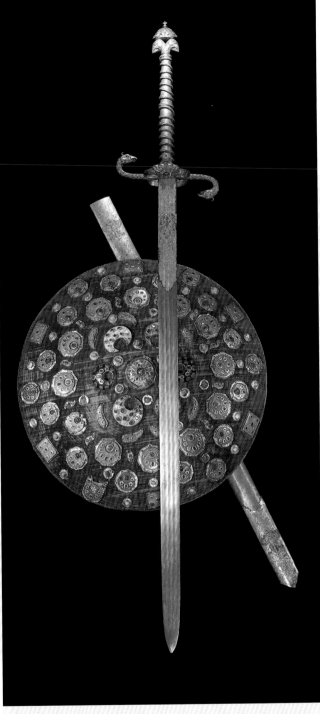

The collection of state regalia is the national pride of Russia. It consists of crowns, sceptres, thrones, the state sword and shield, chains and crosses which played a leading part in court ceremonial from the thirteenth to nineteenth century.

These sacred relics, symbols of state power, were passed down from generation to generation, affirming the continuity and unshakeability of supreme autocracy. They reflect the whole history of the Russian state and were witnesses of the most significant political events.

Cap of Monomach. Orient. Late 13th – early 14th cent. Gold, silver, precious stones, pearls, fur; filigree, seeds of gold, embroidery, chasing, engraving

State sword and shield. Sword – Moscow. Late 17th cent. Silver, steel, gold brocade, wood; casting, chasing, carving, engraving, gilding. Shield – Moscow. Late 17th cent. Gold, silver, precious stones, fabric; casting, chasing, carving, embossing, embroidery

Throne of Ivan the Terrible. Western Europe. 16th cent. Ivory, wood, fabric, metal; ivory carving, casting, gilding

rible's 16th-century Kazan cap-crown, the Great Set consisting of a crown, sceptre and orb made in the 17th century for Tsar Michael Romanov, the cap of Monomach in the Second Set made for Peter I's coronation, and the 1740 crown of Empress Anna Ioan-

Cap-crown of Kazan. Russia. Mid-16th cent. Gold, precious stones, fur; chasing, casting, carving, niello

The special importance of coronations dictated the need for the symbols of power to be fashioned with the utmost richness. Many of them have no equal in world collections in terms of their beauty, fine execution and the rare precious stones that adorn them.

The famous cap of Monomach, a cap-crown of the late 13th to early 14th century, Tsar Ivan the Ter-

Great Set of Tsar Michael Romanov. Crown, sceptre, orb, saadak (quiver and bow case). Late 16th – first third of 17th cent.

Orb and sceptre of Tsar Alexis, son of Michael. Orb – Istambul. Mid-17th century. Gold, precious stones; casting, chasing, engraving, enamelwork. Sceptre – Istambul, 1658. Gold, precious stones; casting, chasing, engraving, enamelwork

Double throne for tsars Ivan and Peter, sons of Alexis. Moscow Kremlin Workshops. 1682–1684. Silver, wood; casting, chasing, carving, gilding

novna are outstanding specimens of the art of jewellery-making.

An important feature of the official ceremonies were the thrones. The oldest throne in the collection dates back to the 16th century, the reign of Tsar Ivan the Terrible. The throne of Tsar Michael Romanov and the Diamond Throne of Tsar Alexis, his son, were used for coronation ceremonies right up to 1896.

Diamond cap-crown of Tsar Ivan, son of Alexis. Moscow Kremlin Workshops. 1680s. Gold, silver, precious stones, pearls, fur; casting, chasing, carving, enamelwork

Diamond cap-crown of Tsar Peter, son of Alexis. Moscow Kremlin Workshops. 1682–1687. Gold, silver, precious stones, pearls, fur; casting, chasing, carving, enamelwork

Throne of Elizabeth, daughter of Peter. St Petersburg. 1740–1742. Wood, fabric; carving, gilding, decorative embroidery

Maltese Crown of Paul I. Late 17th cent. Silver; enamelwork

Full set of ceremonial horse harness. Moscow. 17th cent. Plume, bridle, forehead ornament, jingling chain, neck tassel, saddle, breast ornament. Brocade, precious stones, gold, silver; filigree, chasing

Archak saddle, stirrups, whip. Saddle – Moscow Kremlin Workshops. 1682. Wood, silver, leather, velvet; filigree, enamelwork, gilding, weaving. Stirrups – Moscow Kremlin

Workshops. Second half of 17th cent. Iron, silver; carving, chasing. Whip – Stables Office Workshops. Mid-17th cent. Wood, silver, precious stones, silk, gold thread; chasing, gilding, embroidery

The Armoury possesses one of the world's finest collections of state carriages from the 16th to the 18th centuries, which illustrates the development of carriage-making in Russia and the countries of Western Europe. Fashioned by skilled craftsmen in Russia, Germany, England, France and Austria, they are all interesting for their technical construction and artistic decoration. The oldest item in the collection is an English-made coach presented to Tsar Boris Godunov in 1603 by King James I of England.

The collection of ceremonial horse harness from the 16th to 18th centuries is quite unique. These ex-

Armoury. Room 9. Carriages

Berliner. Belonged to Empress Catherine the Great. St Petersburg. 1769. J.C.Buckendal. Wood, velvet, bronze, paste; painting, gilding, wood-carving, chasing, casting

Summer carriage. England, 1770s. Belonged to Empress Catherine the Great. Maplewood, velvet, bronze; wood carving, oil painting, gilding on gesso

hibits show the great importance attached to state processions and the reception of foreign envoys. The saddles, bridles and other items are lavishly decorated. They are adorned with gold embossing, precious stones, enamelwork, relief chasing, velvety niello and fine engraving. The horse-cloths are made of silk, velvet and brocade and embroidered with pearls and gold and silver thread. Such items were often used for diplomatic gifts. The Armoury has some rare sets of horse harness made by Polish, German, Turkish, Iranian, Chinese and English craftsmen and also some produced in the Caucasus and Central Asia.

The Diamond Fund

In 1967 an exhibition entitled "The Diamond Fund" was opened in the Armoury building. It contained a world-famous collection of precious stones, masterpieces of 18th- and 19th-century jewellery and platinum and gold nuggets. The treasures of the Diamond Fund are part of the national state heritage. Ever since 1922 they have come under the State Valuables Depository (Gokhran).

The nucleus of the collection consists of pieces of jewellery made for the royal court and the Imperial regalia, which were regarded as the property of the Crown, hence the term "crown valuables". The crown valuables were placed in the safekeeping of the state following a decree by Peter the Great in 1719 which declared the regalia to be the pride and glory of Russia. The collection of regalia in the Diamond Fund consists of the Great and Small crowns, maces, sceptres, the Great Chain with the cross and star of the Order of St Andrew the First-Called and clasps to fasten the coronation mantle.

All these items and are of great artistic, historical and material value. They were used almost without changes at all the coronations right up to that of Nicholas II in 1896.

The Great Imperial Crown made in 1762 for the coronation of Catherine the Great by the court jeweller J.Pauzie represents the height of creative imagination, lavish beauty and skilled workmanship. It is adorned with five thousand diamonds arranged in a splendid pattern of laurel wreaths and oak branches. The glitter of the diamonds is enhanced by two rows of gleaming pearls and the crown is topped by a huge red spinel, the second largest in the world, which weighs almost 400 carats.

Military decoration with a portrait of Peter the Great. Early 18th cent. Gold, silver, diamonds, enamelwork

Cross of the Order of St Andrew the First-Called with a detail of the chain. Late 18th cent. Gold, diamonds, enamelwork

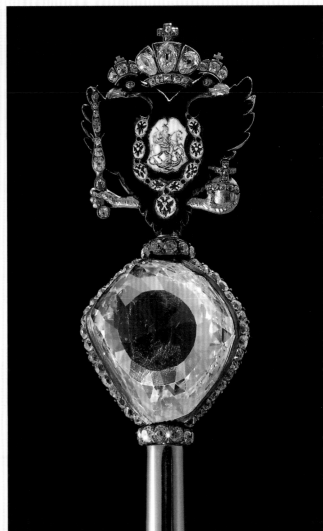

Great and Small imperial crowns, orb and sceptre. Great imperial crown: 1762. St Petersburg. Jeweller J.Pauzie. Gold, silver, diamonds, pearls, spinel. Small imperial crown: 1801. St Petersburg. Jewellers Jakob Duval, Jean Duval. Silver, diamonds. Orb: 1762. St Petersburg. Jeweller G.-F.Eckart. Gold, silver, diamonds, sapphire

Cross of the Order of the Golden Fleece. Mid-19th cent. Gold, silver, diamonds, topazes

Tiara. Circa 1810. Gold, silver, diamonds

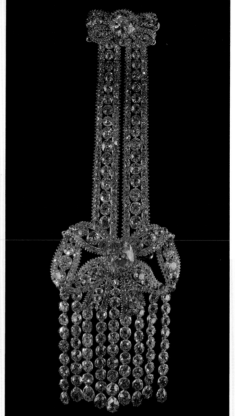

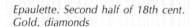

Epaulette. Second half of 18th cent. Gold, diamonds

Porte-bouquet. Circa 1770. Gold, silver, diamonds, enamel

The pride of the collection is the world-famous Orlov diamond, one of the largest faceted diamonds weighing 189 carats. It adorns the sceptre of state.

The pieces of jewellery show a great variety of form, combining sparkling diamonds with red rubies and spinels, blue sapphires and green emeralds. They consist mainly of tiaras, pins, brooches, corsage bouquets and earrings. Each item is a unique work of art.

The seven so-called "historic" stones include the famous Shah diamond. It is particularly valuable for the three inscriptions with the names of its owners and dates, the first being 1591. The diamond was brought to Russia in 1829 together with other gifts from the Shah of Persia to atone for the killing of the Russian envoy in Teheran, Alexander Griboyedov, the author of the play "Wit Works Woe".

Alongside the historical items there are four cases containing modern jewellery made by craftsmen at the Experimental Laboratory of the State Valuables Depository of the Russian Federation. Retaining and

Rose brooch. 1970. V.V.Nikolayev,
G.F.Aleksakhin. Platinum, diamonds

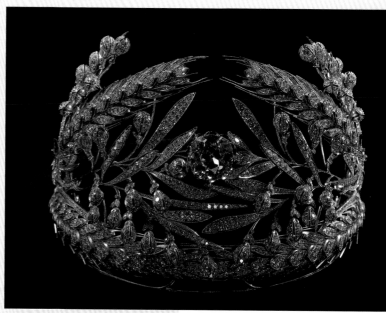

Russian Field tiara. 1980.
V.V.Nikolayev, G.F.Aleksakhin.
Platinum, gold, diamonds

Camel gold nugget. Kolyma. 1947.
Weight 9,288 kg.

Big Triangle gold nugget. Southern
Urals. 1842. Weight 36.2.

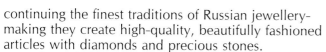

continuing the finest traditions of Russian jewellery-
making they create high-quality, beautifully fashioned
articles with diamonds and precious stones.

Only at the Diamond Fund exhibition can you see
so many large Yakutian faceted diamonds with individual names. They include such giants as the Alexander Pushkin (370-carat), Free Russia (242-carat), and
26th Communist Party Congress (342-carat).

The collection of 20 platinum and 100 gold nuggets is of great value and interest as the only one of
its kind in the whole world.

Arsenal

Arsenal. South facade

The arsenal stands by the Kremlin's west wall between the Trinity and Corner Arsenal towers. Its construction began in 1701 in the reign of Peter the Great who intended it to be not only a storehouse, but also a museum of Russian military glory. The building continued with long intervals right up to 1736. After the terrible Kremlin fire of 1737 the Arsenal was not restored until 1786–1795 under the supervision of Matvei Kazakov. In 1812 it was blown up by the retreating French army. The whole end section of the building from the Corner Arsenal Tower to the Nicholas Tower and the first floor from the Nicholas Tower to the main gate was destroyed by the explosion. In 1815–1828 A.N.Bakarev, I.L.Mironovsky, I.T.Tamansky and E.D.Tyurin restored the Arsenal to the form in which we see it today.

The architectural treatment of the Arsenal is both simple and monumental. The building is trapezoidal in plan with a large inner courtyard and two entrance carriageways made of brick and decorated with white stone.

Old Russian and foreign cannons of artistic value were placed along the Arsenal walls in 1960. Until then they had stood by the old building of the Armoury. The best known of the cannons adorning the Arsenal facade are those made by the eminent Russian armourers A.Chokhov («Troil», 1590) and M.Osipov («Gamayun», 1690).

On either side of the Arsenal entrance arch are memorial plaques, one dedicated to the revolutionary soldiers who died in the Kremlin in October 1917, and the other to Soviet troops who perished in the Kremlin during air raids in the Second World War.

Arsenal. Main facade

"Unicorn" Cannon
by the Arsenal

Senate Palace – Residence of the President of the Russian Federation

Senate Palace – Residence of the President of the Russian Federation

The Senate building is rightly considered a classic example of 18th-century Russian architecture. Designed by Matvei Kazakov, it was built from 1776 to 1787.

The building was intended for various organisations, the most important of which was the Senate, and for meetings of the nobility of Moscow gubernia. In 1856 it was handed over to the Ministry of Justice. After 1918 it housed the Soviet government. Lenin had an apartment and study here, and until recently the Council of Ministers worked here.

The three long blocks of the Senate form a triangle inside which are three inner courtyards. The buildings of the Senate, Arsenal and Armoury (1806–1809) for-

med the new Senate Square in the Kremlin and an interesting classical ensemble. In the middle of the Senate facade is the entrance to the main courtyard. Above the pediment is the dome of the Oval Hall which unites all the parts of the building.

The Senate's main room is the round, blue and white Catherine Hall. The dome is 24.7 metres in diameter and 27 metres high. The hall is adorned with

Senate Palace.
Main Entrance

Senate Palace.
Main Vestibule

columns and 48 bas-reliefs of Russian princes and tsars, as well as scenes representing the deeds of Empress Catherine the Great. At different times it was called the White, Catherine and Sverdlov Hall. After 1919 it was used for holding Communist Party congresses and awarding high state decorations.

The Oval Hall is white and green. After the war it was used for holding meetings of the Council of Ministers of the USSR.

When it was decided to turn the building into the official residence of the President of the Russian Federation, large-scale reconstruction and restoration work was carried out here. As a result the Senate is

113

Senate Palace.
Catherine Hall

Senate Palace.
Armorial Hall

Senate Palace.
Banqueting Hall

115

Senate Palace.
Audience Hall

Senate Palace.
Drawing Room

Mirror with candelabra in the
Drawing Room

Wrought iron gate for entering the grounds of the Senate Palace by the east wall of the Kremlin

Winter Garden in the South Courtyard of the Senate Palace

now called the Senate Palace and here the magnificence of the state halls is combined with the most up-to-date electronic equipment making it possible to govern the vast country from here. The main Catherine Hall is once more decorated with gilt double-headed eagles and the niches now contain statues of "Russia" and "Justice" by A.A.Bichukov. The hall is used for state meetings and receiving foreign delegations.

The Oval Hall is the President's main study. Russians are familiar with the interior from presidential addresses televised here. From the reception vestibule runs is a suite of rooms, each decorated in its own colour. On the third floor is a rest and relaxation area with a small theatre, exhibition halls and the presidential apartments. Also on this floor is the president's library. There are two winter gardens in glass rotundas in the inner courtyards.

Red Square

R ed Square is one of Moscow's most famous sights, combining the churches and civic buildings of six centuries into a single ensemble.

The first reference to trading by the east wall of the Kremlin is in 1434. After the fire of 1493 this area was cleared and no more buildings were erected on it. Later the square was enclosed on the south by St Basil's Cathedral and on the north by the Resurrection Gate in the Kitai-Gorod wall.

After the Saviour Tower was made higher (1625) the space between it, St Basil's and the Rostrum Dias (Lobnoye mesto) began to be called Red (which meant "beautiful") Square. By the end of the seventeenth century this name was used for the whole area from St Basil's to the Resurrection Gate.

Opposite the Saviour Gate in the square is the Rostrum Dias (Lobnoye mesto), first mentioned in the chronicle in 1584. It was a kind of tribune from

Red Square.
View from the Saviour Tower

which the heir to the throne was shown to the people when he reached sixteen, important decrees were proclaimed and sentences for wrongdoers read out.

In the eighteenth century Red Square became a most important ideological and symbolical point in the town. Mass religious ceremonies were held here with the participation of the tsar and patriarch. The tsar's (and later emperor's) processions would enter the square through the Resurrection Gate and then

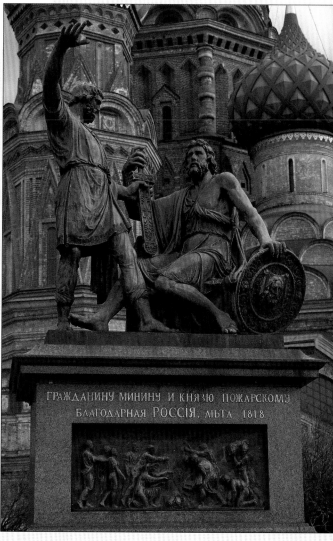

St Basil's (Cathedral of the Intercession-on-the-Moat). 1555–1561

Monument to K.Minin and D.Pozharsky. Sculptor Ivan Martos. 1818

proceed through the Saviour or Nicholas gate into the Kremlin.

A lot of trading still went on in the square as before, however. The first stone trading booths were erected in 1595 on the orders of Boris Godunov. They marked the eastern boundary of Red Square as it is today. These Old Trading Rows were reconstructed between 1786 and 1810 and the New Trading Rows erected along the outer edge of the ditch which went round the Kremlin. The New Trading Rows did not last for long. They collapsed in 1812 when the French blew up the Arsenal as they were retreating from Moscow.

Restoration of the Kremlin walls and towers damaged during the French army's occupation of Moscow began in 1816. The ditch at the foot of the Kremlin walls was filled in and an avenue of limes planted in its place with a boulevard. After the removal of the bastion by the Constantine and Helen Tower the boulevard was continued southwards from the Saviour Gate down Vasilievsky Slope to the Moskva.

In 1818 a monument to K.Minin and D.Pozharsky (sculptor I.P.Martos), the leaders of the people's army of 1612 who liberated Moscow from the Polish interventionists, was unveiled in Red Square in the presence of Alexander I and the whole Imperial family.

In 1883 the large History Museum designed by the architect V.O.Sherwood and the engineer A.A.Semyonov opened its doors to the first visitors.

In place of the trading rows which had become dilapidated by then a new building to house the Upper Trading Rows (now commonly known as GUM, the State Universal Store was built in 1893 to a design by the architect A.N.Pomerantsev and the engineer V.G.Shukhov. This trading complex was then and remains to this day Moscow's largest department store. At the same time a building for the Middle Trading Rows (1889–1891, architect R.I.Klein) was erected not far from St Basil's.

Kremlin Walls. Tsar and Saviour towers with the Lobnoye Mesto (Rostrum Dais) in the foreground

Key to the Saviour Gate. 1833

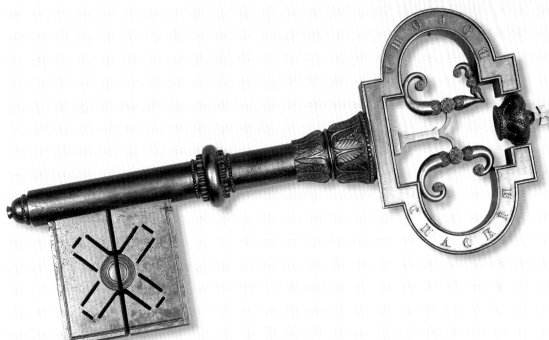

Lenin Mausoleum. 1929–1930.
Architect A.V.Shchusev

Necropolis by the Kremlin wall.
Looking towards the Saviour Tower

When Soviet rule was established in Moscow the funerals of 238 "proletarians who died for the revolution" were held in Red Square by the Kremlin wall. These common graves marked the beginning of a revolutionary necropolis on the spot.

In January 1924, after Lenin's death the first wooden Lenin Mausoleum (architect A.V.Shchusev) was erected in front of the Kremlin's Senate Tower. The mausoleum that replaced it in 1924 was also made of wood. A stone mausoleum was eventually built in 1930, also designed by Shchusev, similar in its architecture to the burial structures of Ancient Egypt and Persia.

Nicholas Tower, State History Museum and Kazan Cathedral from Nikolskaya Street

Resurrection Gate and the Chapel of Our Lady of Iberia

The necropolis by the Kremlin wall was a place of honour for burying those who had performed special services to the state. Such famous people as Yuri Gagarin, the first cosmonaut, Valery Chkalov, the pilot, the eminent physicists I.V.Kurchatov and M.F.Keldysh, the spacecraft designer S.P.Korolyov, the writer Maxim Gorky and famous military leaders such as Marshal G.K.Zhukov are buried here. The necropolis is set apart from the square by the Mausoleum and the stands.

Alexandrovsky Gardens

Alexandrovsky Gardens. View of
the Corner Arsenal Tower

Monument with the names
of great thinkers and revolutionary
socialists. 1918

Main gate to the
Alexandrovsky Gardens

By the eighteenth century the River Neglinnaya, which once protected the Kremlin from the west, was so dirty and shallow that in 1819 the stretch from the Resurrection Gate was confined in a subterranean tunnel and filled in with earth. In 1819–1823 a park was set out on this spot, which was called first the Kremlin, then in 1856 the Alexandrovsky Gardens. The entrance was from Resurrection Square through wrought iron gates.

One of the attractions was the grotto with four classical columns designed by the architect Osip

Grave of the Unknown Soldier
memorial complex by the Kremlin
wall in the Alexandrovsky Gardens.

Opened in 1967. N.V.Tomsky,
D.I.Burdin and others

*Eternal Flame on the Grave of the
Unknown Soldier*

*View of the northwest part of the
Kremlin with the Ivan the Great
Bell-Tower*

Bove which is still standing today on an artificial mound not far from the Middle Arsenal Tower.

A granite obelisk twenty metres high was put up by the main gate in 1913 to mark the tercentenary of the Romanov dynasty. In 1918 it was turned into a monument to outstanding thinkers and revolutionary socialists. In 1967 the obelisk was moved southwards and the Grave of the Unknown Soldier memorial ensemble erected in its place to commemorate the Soviet people's victory in World War II. In the middle is the Eternal Fire of glory and nearby slabs of red porphyry from Soviet hero-cities. A guard of honour post was set up by the Grave of the Unknown Soldier in 1997.

The Moscow Kremlin

Editing
Roza Mikunis,
Alexander Kosseniouk

Photographer
Nikolai Alexeyev

Design
Nikolai Kalinin

Font
Opium New

Red Square
Publishers
109147, Vorontsovskaya 23,
Moscow, Russia
Licence. №063214
May 27, 1999

Printing Karisto
Finland

Fortifications:
1 Saviour Tower
2 Tsar Tower
3 Tocsin Tower
4 Constantine and Helen Tower
5 Beklemishev Tower
6 Peter Tower
7 Second Nameless Tower
8 First Nameless Tower
9 Tainitsky Tower
10 Annunciation Tower
11 Water Tower
12 Borovitsky Tower
13 Armoury Tower
14 Commandant Tower
15 Trinity Tower
16 Trinity Bridge
17 Kutafia Tower
18 Middle Arsenal Tower
19 Corner Arsenal Tower
20 Nicholas Tower
21 Senate Tower

Kremlin monuments, etc.
22 Assumption Cathedral
23 Church of the Deposition of the Robe
24 Annunciation Cathedral
25 Hall of Facets
26 Archangel Cathedral
27 Ivan the Great Bell-Tower ensemble
28 Church of the Twelve Apostles
29 Patriarchal Palace
30 Terem churches and Tsarina's Golden Chamber
31 Terem Palace
32 Churches of the Resurrection of Lazarus and the Nativity of the Virgin
33 Great Kremlin Palace
34 Armoury
35 Poteshny Palace
36 State Kremlin Palace
37 Arsenal
38 Senate Palace – residence of the President of the Russian Federation
39 Administrative building
40 Lenin Monument (removed in 1995)
41 Tainitsky Gardens
42 Tsar Bell
43 Tsar Cannon
44 Ivan Square
45 Cathedral Square

Around the Kremlin
46 Red Square
47 Lenin Mausoleum
48 Stands by the Mausoleum

The Moscow Kremlin in 1971.
Drawing by A.Khamtsov